It was Hot!

Illustrated by Karen Bell

High-Frequency Words			
was	he	a	the

Scott
Foresman

Editorial Offices: Glenview, Illinois • Parsippany, New Jersey • New York, New York
Sales Offices: Parsippany, New Jersey • Duluth, Georgia • Glenview, Illinois
Coppell, Texas • Ontario, California

The sun was hot.

Diz was hot.

Diz got in.

He got wet.

A | bug | got | in.

The bug got wet.

It was fun.